Arachnid or Insect?

by Kristin Cashore

Scott Foresman
is an imprint of

Glenview, Illinois • Boston, Massachusetts • Chandler, Arizona
Upper Saddle River, New Jersey

Every effort has been made to secure permission and provide appropriate credit for photographic material. The publisher deeply regrets any omission and pledges to correct errors called to its attention in subsequent editions.

Unless otherwise acknowledged, all photographs are the property of Scott Foresman, a division of Pearson Education.

Photo locators denoted as follows: Top (T), Center (C), Bottom (B), Left (L), Right (R), Background (Bkgd)

3 (TR), (BL) ©Jody Dole/The Image Bank/Getty Images, (TL), (CL), (CR), (BR) ©Edwin L Wisherd/National Geographic/Getty Images; 5 (C) ©James Cotier/Stone/Getty Images; 8 (TL) ©Luis Castaneda Inc/The Image Bank/Getty Images, (BC) ©Darlyne A Murawski/ National Geographic/Getty Images; 9 ©Geoff Du Feu/Taxi/Getty Images 10 (TL) ©Bettmann/CORBIS, (TR) ©Darlyne A Murawski/National Geographic/Getty Images, (BC) ©Stone/Getty Images

ISBN 13: 978-0-328-50838-9
ISBN 10:   0-328-50838-1

5 6 7 8 9 10 V010 13 12

Many people believe that all bugs and creepy crawly things are insects. This is not true!

A spider is not an insect. It is an arachnid.

What is the difference?

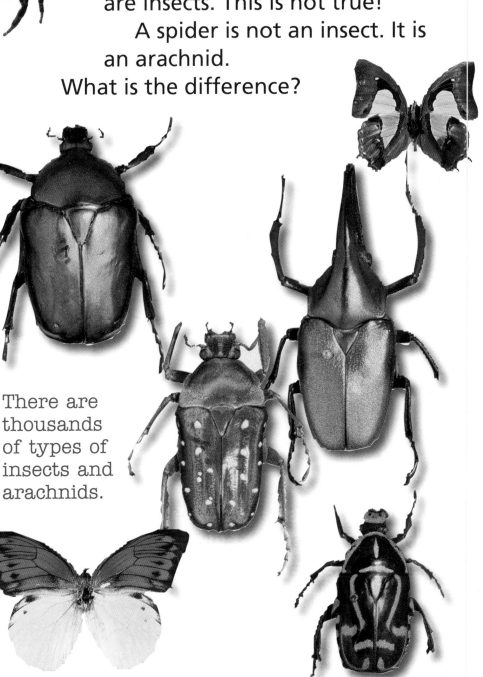

There are thousands of types of insects and arachnids.

3

Insects

All insects have six legs. An ant has six legs.

All insects have a body in three parts. An ant has a body in three parts.

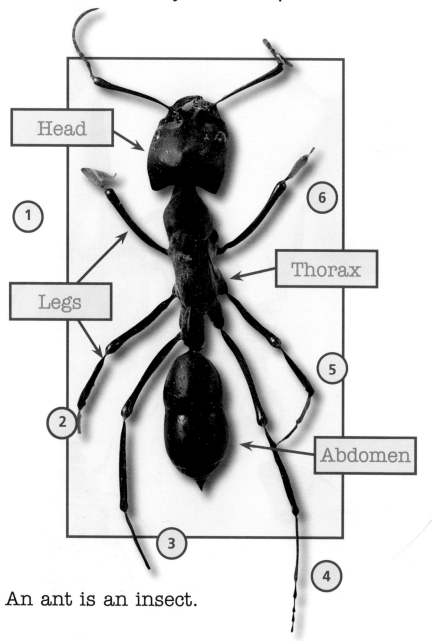

Head

Legs

Thorax

Abdomen

An ant is an insect.

A fly is an insect.

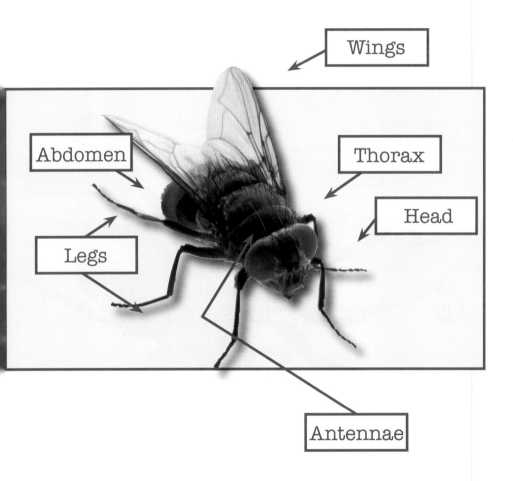

All insects have antennae. Antennae are found on an insect's head. Insects use them to feel and smell.

Not all insects have wings, but many do.

5

Arachnids

An arachnid can be tiny, just like an insect. Arachnids and insects are different, though.

All arachnids have eight legs, not six. An arachnid's body is in two parts, not three.

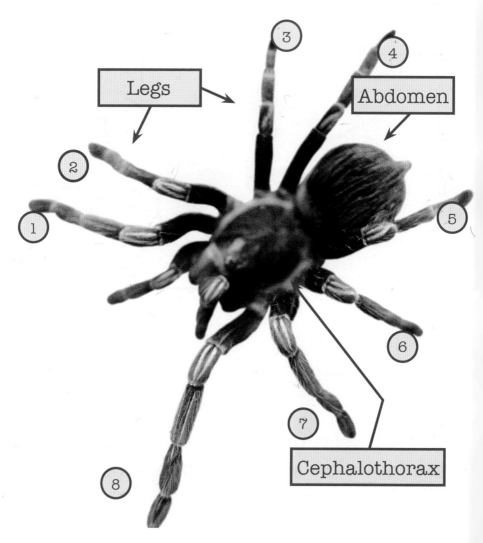

A spider is an arachnid.

Arachnids never have antennae.
Arachnids never have wings.

Spiders spin
beautiful webs with
their own silk.

A dragonfly is an insect.

A grasshopper is an insect.

A butterfly is an insect.

Finally, a ladybug is an insect.

Dragonfly

Butterfly

Grasshopper

Look for legs. Look for wings. Look for antennae. Are these insects?

A ladybug hides its wings under its red shell.

Ladybugs have a hard shell over their wings. This keeps them safe from other animals.

Ladybugs also play dead to keep themselves from being caught. They lie still and do not move. Other animals leave the ladybug alone!

A tick is an arachnid.

A mite is an arachnid.

Finally, a scorpion is the biggest arachnid!

Spiders are not the only arachnids.

Spider

Tick

Mite

Many scorpions
live in the desert.

Scorpions can be eight inches long.

Scorpions keep themselves safe in a special way. They have poison in their tails! If a scorpion is attacked, it will sting. Whatever you do, do not pick one up!

Insects and arachnids have always been easy to mix up. You will not mix them up anymore!

If you see a bug today or tomorrow, count its legs. Count the parts of its body. Check for antennae. Check for wings. Now will you know which it is—insect or arachnid?